Survival: How to Survive Successfully

Bushcraft Skills, Disaster Prepping, Foraging, and Urban Survival

Table of Contents

Introduction

I would like to thank you for purchasing this book. Trouble has the odd habit of finding us at the worst times and if you're not prepared it can be disasterous. Most of the issues that we encounter on a daily basis are easily resolved however, there may come a time when we need to be more prepared for dangerous and potentially life threatening situations. This book is a guide that contains information on prepping and survival when disaster strikes.

Prepping isn't something that can be done overnight. It requires planning, preparation, courage and both mental and physical strength. The four major aspects that this book contains are bushcraft skills, disaster prepping, foraging, and urban survival.

Please understand that reading this book alone will not be enough if you don't take action and practice.

Chapter 1: All About Prepping

What is prepping

Prepping simply means preparation. It is to be prepared for any disaster. Disasters can occur naturally such as earthquakes, tornados, or floods, and they can be manmade as well such as acts of terrorism or riots. Prepping will give you three major advantages during the time of a disaster. When disaster strikes people tend to rush to the supermarkets, hardware stores and pharmacies hoping to grab everything that they feel they need and more often than not, come up short.

The problem is that the supply at these stores is limited and their demand increases tremendously during these times. So, the supply falls short of the demand. The chances of you forgetting essentials is highly likely due to the chaos and panic that you may be feeling. Going back to the store might not be an option though. Prepping would ensure that you have all the supplies that you might need on hand at a moment's notice.

As soon as disaster strikes you can have all the supplies handy in your kit and this will increase your chances of survival tremendously. Another issue is that there might be power losses that could have a detrimental effect on your survival. If you are well prepared than you can easily continue on without it.

We have become more dependent on technology and power more than we ever were. We tend to take these things for granted as they become more integrated into our everyday lives. In a situation where you don't have access to either of these things, you might feel overwhelmed and lost. If you have prepared beforehand then you can face the problems better.

We are not only dependent on technology and equipment but also on the other basic necessities like food and water. During a crisis, we might have to go days without these necessities. If you have backup supplies handy then you will be better prepared. Prepping is neither hard nor is it expensive. It just requires some effort in the form of practice and planning. It also requires organizational skills such as control and coordination. Prepping isn't a new fad. It has been around in one form or another for centuries. During the times of war people would stock up on all the essential supplies like canned foods, dried fruits, vegetables, dry goods, and toiletries.

Preppers believe that they are responsible for their own safety and security and they believe in self-reliance. Prepping consists of two steps. The first one is mental prepping and the second one is physical prepping. Mental prepping consists of building your confidence, courage, and willpower, for surviving. The physical preparation requires that you build up the proper stamina and energy.

Chapter 2: The Basic Skills of Survival

There is a lot of information that is available about basic survival skills, all that information might seem overwhelming. In this chapter let's take a look at the six basic skills that are required for survival.

Attitude matters

More than any other skill of survival, your attitude will determine how high your chances for survival are. This is the first of the basic skills and it can even determining whether you live or die. The simple rule of threes will provide you the guidelines to prioritize your survival skills. The rules of threes are that a human being can live without air for 3 minutes, without regulated body temperature for 3 hours, without water for 3 days and 3 weeks without food. Shelter should be at the top of your list, followed by water, and then food. Whenever you are faced with a situation where your survival is at stake, then remember this abbreviation SPEAR, it means Stop, Plan, Execute, Assess and the Reevaluate. When you systematically follow the above-mentioned steps then you can keep your mind as well as your body actively occupied. If you keep a positive attitude even when the times get tough, the chances of your survival will improve.

Shelter

Most of those who are forced into a situation that threatens their survival often get into trouble because of their direct exposure to the harsh elements. In any survival situation it is of important to build or find a suitable shelter. It is important minimize the loss of warmth or water if you happen to be stuck in an arid region. Some of the things that you will need to think about while building shelter are location, insulation, heat source and whether or not you should opt for personal or group shelter. There are different types of shelters to chose from they could be natural shelters such as a cave, a hollow stump or log and building shelters such as a debris hut.

Water

Up to 78% of the human body is made up of water and therefore it is no surprise that water is one of the most essential items for survival. The human body requires about a gallon of water per day. Dehydration and the pathogens from untreated water can easily kill just as quickly as the elements. When stuck in wilderness the best sources of clean drinking water would be springs, water streams, and morning dew. You can purify water by boiling it, by making use of any herbal treatment or even chemicals are a good option. There are also portable filters that can be used to purify water. If you can maintain a positive attitude, create shelter and obtain some clean water then you can successfully survive for a few weeks.

Fire

This isn't a direct survival need, but a fire is one of the basic survival skills. It cannot only help you stay warm if needed, but it can also help you dry out your clothes, boil water, and cook food. It can also provide the much needed psychological support by making you feel secure and safe. You need to carry a couple of fire starting tools in your survival kit like a lighter, match box, flint and steel. Even with these tools it can be quite difficult to light a fire due to the different elements. So, you will need to practice how to make a fire in any weather.

Food

It might surprise you to see food this low on the list of basic things you need to survive. According to the rule of threes, a human being can go without food for three weeks, this might not be something that you would want to test. Thankfully most of the natural environments we may be surrounded in has edible items that can help you meet your nutritional requirements. You need to be able to identify plants properly before you try consuming them, because there are poisonous plants as well. Some of the edible plants that are in abundance in North America are cattail, conifers, grasses, and oaks. If you are not able to identify any particular plant, then its better that you stay away from it.

Naturalist skills

The more you know about nature, the chances of your survival will improve. You need to be able to understand various nature skills if you want to survive. For instance, wildlife tracking skills would come in handy if you are trying to locate wild game for food and if you have knowledge of herbal plants, you will be able to treat various illnesses as well. Naturalist knowledge will prove to be invaluable especially in those situations where you have to survive for prolonged periods of time.

With these six basic survival skills, you can easily sustain yourself in the outdoors.

Chapter 3: Getting Started with Bushcraft

To put it simply, bushcraft is the study of nature and the resources that nature provides us with. Some of the resources that are available in the nature are quite obvious and they don't require any knowledge to access them, then there are resources that require a large amount of knowledge or skill like building a canoe from birch bark. Given the various concepts that are included in bushcraft, it might seem a little overwhelming to a beginner. Let's go through this one concept at a time.

Start with the basis

The most important of outdoor skill would be lighting a fire. When you are learning to light a fire you will also learn to not only identify different species of trees but also their burning properties. You will learn which plants and trees would make good tinder and kindling. Some of the techniques like feather sticks for instance require a lot of practice at honing at your carving skills. More often than not, people who are interested in bushcraft don't spend enough time refining their fire lighting skills. This isn't something that can be rushed. It takes a while to get the hang of it.

Bushcraft gear

There is no such thing as bushcraft equipment. There is equipment that is being associated with bushcraft these days. This is completely unnecessary. Most of this so-called bushcraft equipment is just glorified camping equipment. When your bushcraft skills get better, you will need less equipment in your kit.

The Hadza are a native tribe of Tasmania, the members of this tribe are known for their exceptional bushcraft skills, they virtually own no equipment whatsoever. They are exceptionally skilled without any special equipment. Things like the composition of the steel of the knife or a blade with scandi grind wouldn't make any difference to the Hadza. So, you need to think more like the Hadza and less like a shopping addict.

What you need for getting started

If you ever go camping outdoors, then you would probably have some outdoor clothes. You might have a waterproof jacket. This is one of the essentials to help you last a day or so in the woods. If you probably want to stay a little longer, then as a beginner it is advisable that you carry a few extra things. If you carry some basic camping equipment you are all set, you don't need anything fancy. A tent, a sleeping bag, probably a can of baked beans or anything that can be heated over a small fire, bottle of water and a box of matchsticks would do. It doesn't take much to actually survive with these few skill, ingenuity, and using nature's resources.

Most of the bushcraft techniques can be made much easier with the help of a really basic cutting tool. Buy a cheap yet durable knife, just like the Hadza. As a beginner you can make use of a knife or even a basic pruning saw would be helpful until you develop your knife skills. A small saw will definitely make things much easier and safer than a knife.

Start working on your bushcraft skills

Lighting fires is the first step and being able to light fire with a small flame is really a valuable skill to know. You can start practicing with matches and then you can practice in rain. Then you can move onto lighting fires by making use of natural materials by the means of sparks. This will help you gain a better understanding of the materials that would catch fire with just the help of a spark, burst into flames or just smolder. Then you can make use of natural material to start a fire with the smoldering materials.

10 areas that you need to focus on

Bushcraft can be broken down into 10 basic categories and then you can add on to it as you get a better grip on your skills.

Fire craft: It isn't rocket science to start a fire using a lighter, matches, and some lighter fluid. But how will you start a fire when you don't have these materials? Using flint, organic materials, and other naturally found materials are going to be the tools of choice the longer you're in the woods. Fire craft is concerned with starting and maintaining fires regardless of the conditions you are in. This includes the usage of multiple techniques such as using flint, sun, smoldering plants, how to make use of fire for survival and also to transport the fire you have made from one location to another without having to start all over again.

Tracking: it really is useful to be good at tracking. This will prove to be a great way to catch food. Apart from this also it is important because it will let you track people and animals to see if any particular campsite was being frequented by any animals or if people have been through there before. Animals and human beings tend to stick to familiar paths and they would follow the same paths every time. This will help you set snares, procure water, and avoid certain areas.

Hunting: This one is pretty obvious, isn't it? It is not just about being able to hunt with hunting rifles but about making use of a variety of tools. You won't have access to any of these in the wilderness. Trapping is the most common manner of hunting small game in the wilderness. It is not just about trapping but you should also know about how you want to handle what you trap and hunt once you have trapped it. Butchering and skinning techniques will come in handy if you want to eat what you have caught.

Fishing: Learning to fish is a handy skill. Fish is a good source of protein and fat. You should learn how to fish by making use of a variety of equipment. Line and hook and trapping are the two basic methods of learning how to fish. If you have materials and also your ability to set traps, then trapping is the best method.

Foraging: Fishing and trapping animals is good but this won't be sufficient to survive if you aren't able to build a fire to cook your catch on. So, foraging is just as important. You need to learn about the plants that are suitable for consumption and the ones that aren't. The first thing that you need to do is get familiar with all the plants and trees that exist in your surroundings and are safe to be consumed.

Shelter Building: It is really important that you can build a proper shelter, because it will not only keep you dry and warm, but also potentially keep you safe from predators. Keeping dry is really important because it will prevent you from getting sick and keep your equipment usable. It is important that you not only know how to build basic shelter but also know how to do this by making use of a variety of resources.

Knives and Axes: Bladed implements are some of the most essential tools to bushcraft. Survival knives and axes can be vital for survival and you should be able to use and care for your equipment properly. You don't need heavy-duty knives. You will need small and durable knives. You need to learn how to use these tools properly and sharpen, repair, and maintain them as well.

Wood Carving: We often make use of a lot of wooden implements without even realizing it. Wooden spoons and handles for knives are some of the commonly used wooden tools. These skills require patience and practice to be able to successfully make these items. Get this practice in before you need to use it in a survival situation.

Container Construction: Another important skill that you should learn would be making containers for storing food, clothes, and tools as well. We are used to just walking into a store, picking up a container, and using them until they break and then we repeat the process all over again. The bushcraft way of doing things is different. You will start respecting these containers more when you have to make them by yourself. It is important to learn how to make use of a variety of materials like woods, leather, metal, and some odd materials like tire rubber as well. You can also make a waterproof container by making use of tarp or by applying melted wax to containers or buckets as well.

Rope Craft: If you were a Boy or Girl Scout you may be familiar with rope craft and tying knots. Rope craft comes in handy whenever you want to tie your tent, preparing snares, and also for quick release knots while climbing. While learning to do this, take a look at how you can make rope by making use of naturally available fibers.

Chapter 4: Managing Disasters

Disasters don't give a notice before striking, they often cannot be. The best you can do is be prepared for them so that you are better equipped to deal with them. This chapter gives a brief overview of what you should do in case a disaster strikes. Disasters can be both natural and manmade. For instance, earthquakes, tsunamis, volcanic eruptions, and tornadoes are natural disasters and terrorism and riots are manmade disasters.

Earthquakes

An earthquake can be recognized by the shaking of the ground. Head out towards an open space without any buildings, electrical poles, or trees and stay put when an earthquake occurs. If you are indoors, then crawl under a sturdy desk, table, or bed to reduce the chances of debris falling on you. If not, you can sit against a wall with your knees up and your head tucked in between your knees. This is done to ensure that no debris hits your head. If you happen to live in an area that is prone to earthquakes, then you should make use of lightweight material for the purpose of construction. Also ensure that you avoid or keep the usage of glass as decoration as minimal as possible.

Heat Waves

When the temperature of the area you reside in starts increasing at a rapid and high rate that's the indication of a heat wave. Heat waves usually occur in arid regions and they can result in loss of water due to extreme heat. The loss of water due to soaring temperatures can do damage to flora and fauna. Get shelter and try to go outside as little as possible during a heat wave. If you reside in an area that is prone to heat waves then the materials used for construction should be tough and you should seal your house completely when you know a heat wave is about to approach. Ensure that there is sufficient water stored in the house. A heat wave can bring draught along with it and you should stock up on plenty of water. Store preserved foods and turn on cooling equipment during this period.

Volcano

Volcanic eruptions cannot be recognized easily and volcanoes are of three types. You need to know the category of volcano the mountain or the hill that is located in your region is. If such a volcano happens to be an active volcano, you can recognize an oncoming volcanic eruption through the erratic behavior of animals because they usually flee and are more sensitive towards these things. In case of an eruption, it is better if you stay indoors because the risk of a building burning down is quite low depending on the construction of your home. You should shut and seal all the windows, doors, and openings and also wear some protective gear to ensure that you don't inhale the poisonous fumes. Store sufficient water in your house and keep all your supplies away from the walls. There is a misconception that if you reside in a high rise building then the volcanic ash wouldn't reach you. This is wrong because volcanic ash is known to reach great heights. Therefore, it would be wise to stay indoors.

Hurricanes

When a low-pressure zone is created around water bodies it usually causes hurricanes. This results in high velocity winds and torrential rainfall. If you live near the coastline or have a house overlooking a water body, then you can recognize an oncoming hurricane by checking the movement of water. Also keep tuning into your local weather channel to see if a hurricane has been predicted. Animals tend to move away from the coast and head inland, even this behavior is a sign of an impending disaster. In case of a hurricane you can expect power outages and you need to stock up on all the basic amenities like food, water, medicine, batteries, candles, flashlights, and toiletries. If you can, get away from your house and reach a higher level ground. If the water body starts to flood or a flashflood occurs, you won't have any time to act. Carry satellite phones since even during any network problems, these will still work and will help you communicate. You should always carry your survival kit with you.

Land Slides

Landslide can occur at any point of time in hilly and mountainous regions. Landslides are sudden, but rainfalls and avalanches usually result in landslides. In case of a landslide, you have only two options, either stay indoors or flee. Preferably it's better if you don't travel during heavy rains and seek shelter when the rain begins. If you can't avoid travelling in chilly weather, then you should carry sufficient salt because this will help in melting the snow. The steps that you take in case of an earthquake will help in the case of a landslide as well. Head towards an open space or seek refuge under a sturdy table or bed to avoid debris. Ensure that your emergency supplies will last you for at least a few days.

Tsunamis

The enormous waves that occur due to disturbances under the surface of the water like volcanic eruptions, earthquakes, or even landslides may result in tsunamis. Tsunamis are also referred as seismic sea waves. The waves in a tsunami can be over 100 feet high and can travel at a speed of more than 100 miles per hour. Tsunamis might not hit all the coasts in a similar manner but they are all very dangerous. If either a major earthquake or a landslide occurs close to the shore, then the first wave of tsunami can hit the coastline without warning. So, it would be a good idea to plan in advance to ensure the safety of yourself, your family, and property. Make survival kits and keep one in your car in case you have to flee on a moment's notice. Make sure that you know the height of the area you reside in and its distance from the coastline. If you are a tourist then you should familiarize yourself with the tsunami evacuation warnings. When a tsunami warning is issued you should evacuate immediately and head for higher ground away from the shore. Head to public shelter when the evacuation warning is issued and only head back after the officials have issued an order stating that it is safe to return. Stay away from areas that were hit and debris.

Chapter 5: Foraging

Foraging for plants

In today's world we have become dependent on the supermarkets and various stores for providing us with food. The environment is becoming extremely unstable. Due to that, it is in our best interest to be prepared for any impeding dangers that might be lurking right around the corner. During the times of a disaster, you might not be able to find food that is edible and your emergency supplies might run low. Because of this, foraging is a valuable skill.

Foraging is the method by which you can search for edible foods. Foraging is primarily associated with forests or other outdoor areas where you don't have access to other supplies. People in earlier times would need to search for food and then move on to another area once they have exhausted the food supplies in that area. Foraging isn't restricted to just searching for edible, but it also includes foraging for water, hunting, and fishing as well. One thing you need to remember about foraging is that you are eating for your survival. It is a good idea to carry canned foods and stock up on emergency supplies.

The most important skill when it comes to foraging is your ability to identify whether or not a plant is edible or poisonous. This can be a matter of life or death. The one thing that you need to do is familiarize yourself with plants in your area and learn about their properties. When you are trying to survive after a disaster strikes, you should to stay without familiar areas. This isn't the time to explore uncharted territories unless you absolutely need to. The reason is that the plant species that you might find elsewhere would be different from what you are familiar with. Learn about the various species of plants in your vicinity and read about identifying different plants that are harmful and poisonous. IIf you can't identify a plant then it is a good idea to stay away from it. When you are learning to identify plants, you should also look into what their various uses are.

You need to get yourself acquainted with herbs, bushes, and trees. You can also take classes on gardening or courses that are dedicated to help you identify different plants. Learn about different plants, if they are edible or their associated medicinal benefits. Some plants tend to look similar but if you cannot identify a plant 100% then you should probably avoid it. It might end up being a poisonous plant. Remember that you should check and recheck the plants before deciding whether or not it is edible. Also learn about the different soil conditions because certain species are confined to a particular soil type.

You should also make it a point to learn the scientific names of the plants because several plants might have the same common name, if not the scientific names then learn their Latin names. To identify a plant there are a couple of things that you should do. First step would be to observe the plant closely, take a look at its flowers, leaves, and roots.

If you cannot even vaguely identify the plan by now, then it is better to just avoid such a plant. Second step would be to take a sniff of the plant. Don't get too close, just get a whiff. See if you can identify it. Third step would be to touch and feel the texture of the plant. Examine the flowers, leaves and stems. Finally, if you are 100% sure that the plant isn't poisonous, take a small bite of it. Remember to rinse it before eating it. Don't gobble down a handful of leaves, eat one leaf or petal and see whether or not you have developed any allergic reactions. Rub the leaf or the petal on your skin and wait. If you notice any reaction, then stay away from it. Also learn about the natural habitats of different plants.

In case you get lost, then you might be able to figure out your location by identifying plants. You should also learn about the various seasons in which a particular plant grows, because particular varieties might be restricted to a particular season. If you can afford to light a fire, then it will be best to boil the plant, roots, leaves, stem, and flowers to get rid of any harmful bacteria. In some plants, it is safe to consume only specific parts. So the knowledge of this can literally make the difference between life and death. Do not forage in areas that may have been contaminated by chemicals or other toxic elements. If the fruit bearing trees are near roads, then the fruits of such tress might be contaminated with lead and you can risk lead poisoning. Also if a plant looks sick, dying, or infected with insects or just not healthy then stay away from it.

Foraging for Water

Like I have mentioned earlier water is very important for survival. Dehydration can lead to death. Even when you manage to obtain water, you need to be cautious to ensure that the water is safe to drink. In the wilderness your chances of survival will depend greatly on obtaining water. The freshest sources of water must be used. Don't use water from any water bodies that are situated near industries or factories. If this happens to be the only source of water then remember to filter it before consumption. Filtering pumps and chemicals like iodine can be used. In case of a survival situation always remember to carry these. Pocket sized filters with little to no maintenance required can be easily stowed in a survival kit.

The other option is that you boil the water before consuming it. You can also make your own water purifier in less than ten minutes. All you need are two soda bottles and a plastic tube. Drill a hole in the cap of each bottle and insert the tube into these holes. Place these bottles a few feet apart. One bottle should be places in the sun and the other in shade. The sunrays will heat up the water and the vapor will rise and get transferred into the other bottle. Always remember to carry a few bottles of water in your survival kit.

Basics of fishing

Learning how to fish can be a valuable skill in a survival situation, because fish is high in proteins as well as healthy fats and oils. In a survival situation it is highly unlikely that you will have fishing gear readily with you. Here are some basic ways you can fish with the use of traditional fishing equipment. You can fishing spears. You can fashion a spear out of almost anything. You just need a long stick and mount a sharp piece of bone, metal or even wood to make the pointed tip. This method is most effective when fishing in shallow water and it is easy to catch bigger fish with it. You need to have a lot of patience and practice. A fish weir can also be used. You just need to create a fence in shallow water. There needs to be one entrance through which the fish can enter but no exit. The next option would be catching fish by hand, using fishing nets, or just by stunning them. It is not just about catching fish, but you should also know how to cook what you have caught. Cooking fish on fire is a good idea or you can also steam it in some water.

Basics of hunting

Tracking is not as easy as you think it would be and you need to look out for certain basic things. The first rule of tracking is that you need to slow down and just use your eyes. You need to look out for footprints. You need to learn how to identify various types of tracks, so that you can decide whether it is something that might be your prey or something that you should avoid. Going after what you think is a deer and running into a bear will quickly turn you from the hunter into the hunted.

If you happen to be in a grassy area, you may be able to see trails that are running through grass. The thing that you need to look out for is a shine. A shine is what happens when the grass has been bent and will reflect light much differently than that reflected by the rest. Also look for flagging, when an animal moves through grass then the grass tends to bend in the direction of the travel. This will provide you a clear idea of which direction the animal is moving in. Depending on the animal, this will be your cue to follow it or go in the opposite direction.

Hunting also seems quite simple, doesn't it? First thing that you need to be mindful of is the wind direction. Animals can smell way better than us and if they catch a whiff of you then you'll have a hard time catching anything. Always ensure that the wind is in your favor. Keep a low profile. Make sure that you don't make any abrupt movements and that you move slowly. You don't have to charge at the animal, just keep a low profile and try to move without making too much noise. Animals tend to have a keener sense of sound than most human beings, so you will have to stay quiet. Keep calm and stay patient. It could take a while before you can either trap the prey or get a shot off at it.

Chapter 6: Urban Survival

To survive in an urban environment, you will have to make use of what you have learned so far and a few other skills. The urban survival techniques and objectives are much different from the survival skills that you would have to use in the wild. There are a number of reality shows that focus on survival in the wilderness. In most of these shows either the participants are given plenty of supplies to reach the end task or just a tool to survive in the wilderness. These shows do showcase various survival situations in the wilderness but in reality these shows represent such aspects of survival that hardly matter in the urban setting. Survival skills such as hunting, fishing, foraging for plants, and building shelter are all important but have virtually no value for urban survival. Things like situational awareness, personal protection, planning and preparing for a disaster are more important for surviving in an urban scenario. Urban survival scenarios can be divided into two distinct categories. The first is the individual adverse event such as robbery, mugging, or even carjacking. The other category is a large-scale survival event, such as riots, natural disasters, or even the collapse of an economy. The likelihood of finding yourself in one of these situations is very real and therefore it is essential that you are prepared to deal with them.

Urban survival is dependent on the application and use of six principles and these are planning, preparation, training, protection, communication, and safe haven. In this chapter we will take a look at these principles so that you can prepare yourself for any unpleasant event that can occur in an urban setting.

Planning

Planning is an important managerial skill and the success of any project would depend upon how good a plan is. Without a plan, you won't have any direction, objectives, and no way to document your progress. For obtaining success you need to set goals and objectives. In this case, the goal would be preparing for and training to survive any form of urban survival scenarios. You need to have two general sets of plans. The first one would be to suit your individual as well as unique situations. The first plan would be set all the survival tools in one place to prepare for an urban emergency. The second step would be to make smaller plans that you need to develop to ensure that everyone in your family knows about the procedures to follow in case of a crisis. You need to develop four separate plans, a plan to deal with natural disasters, one for getting out of the town, a plan in case of a fire, and a home invasion or robbery plan. Each of these plans would have different elements but one thing that is common to all these plans is to ensure that everyone in your family is safe even in a critical situation.

Preparation

Preparation can ensure success and in a survival situation it can mean the difference between living and dying. This is probably one of the hardest things related to urban survival. We are accustomed to having everything well within our reach that we tend to keep postponing the preparation aspect. However, in the case of an urban survival situation it is highly likely that you will be cut off from your regular supply of essential commodities such as food, water, and clothing for an extended period of time. It is easy to keep telling yourself that nothing like this would happen to you, but a disaster a can strike at any given point of time. So it is really important that you are prepared. You need to ensure that you have stocked up on enough food, propane for cooking and heating, water is stored in tubs or even rain barrels and also ensure that you have tools for personal protection. Also stock up on some fuel in case of an emergency evacuation.

Training and Practice

There are several areas in which you should get some training in. You should take courses on situation awareness, self-defense, obtain a license for carrying a weapon, first aid training, and physical fitness. You should be trained in each of these areas and this will add to your preparation and ability to manage any urban survival situation with less stress. It is not enough to just be trained but you should also keep practicing what you have learned. You need to keep practicing these skills if you want to remain competent. Keep having mock drills to carry out the plans you have drafted. If need be then you can make the necessary changes.

Protection

Whether it happens to be a large-scale disaster scenario or an isolated incident, protection is a key aspect for your survival. The aspects where protection is essential are you, your family, your home, and your travel needs. It can be quite easy to forget this, but you need to protect yourself first before you try and protect others. If you are injured or killed, then you can't protect your family. Carjackings, home invasions, and robberies occur when you aren't expecting them. In situation like this you need to stay calm and maintain a sense of situational awareness. Being prepared is critical for your survival. In some scenarios where a natural disaster strikes, it is immediately followed by looting or civil unrest. In situations like this it is important for you to stay in your protection mode. You need to be aware of the situation you are in and use your personal protection skills to survive.

Ensure that you have easy access to your tools in any of the urban survival situations. In case of a situation where you need to move from one place to another, then vigilance and attention to your surroundings is key to your survival.

Communication

One of the first concerns of any of the family members are the whereabouts of their loved ones. You might have come across articles in the news where people stuck in a disaster zone or even in the case of a home fire are trying to determine or locate where the other members of their family are. This is a very common occurrence. In today's world we are lucky enough to have cell phones that let us communicate from anywhere. In case of an emergency where the lines of communication are down, you should always carry a satellite phone.

Safe Haven

A safe haven is a place that you have chosen where you and your family can be safe. You should decide on two safe havens. The first one should be within your home or residence, a room where you and your family members can regroup to protect yourself from any imminent threat. The second one should be any location that you can go to that will provide you protection. A safe room can be a simple room or it can be a panic room with steel reinforcements that contains sufficient supplies of food, water, protective tools, and several devices to facilitate communication. You and your family need to decide on the locations that can be ideal safe havens and everyone should be aware of the multiple routes that can be taken in case of any blockades.

Chapter 7: Essential Urban Skills

If you live in a city, then the urban survival skills are capable of saving your life during any major disaster. In this chapter we will take a look at the nine essential urban skills. These skills aren't given in any particular order.

Water procurement and purification

This is an invaluable skill to learn, for your survival in both wilderness and in the city as well. The water is more likely to be contaminated in the city so you need to make sure that you know of multiple ways in which you can purify the water. Depending on the area that you reside in, it might be comparatively difficult to find water than it would be in the wilderness. Even if you happen to live near any water body such as a lake or a pond, getting to and going back form it might be really dangerous because of other individuals who might also flock to the same water body to quench their thirst. To get around this, you should consider harvesting rainwater and you can also dig your own well.

Security and awareness

When a disaster strikes, the police forces in the city may be stretched to their limit and you can also expect the crime rate to escalate potentially, especially if the city or town is running out of food supply. There are different ways in which you can make your home secure and also deter potential burglars from entering. You should also practice your general awareness skills. You need to be alert all the time and start taking note of people around you. For instance observe if someone is watching or following you. You should watch out for things that seem out of ordinary like any suspicious vehicles that are parked outside your home and listen carefully for any unusual sounds such as shouting or running or even smells like smoke or gasoline. You need to be aware of the exits that you can take in case you have to run. It takes time and practice as well to reach a heightened state of awareness. It might seem like paranoia to you but it could save your life.

Combat and self defense

Even though you may have a state of the art security system at home and a great sense of awareness, this will not help you if you come face to face with a mugger or a burglar outside of your home. It is a good idea to have a gun or other weapon that you feel comfortable with for the purpose of self-defense. Make sure to check your area's laws on what you can own or carry. You may not be able to access your weapon quickly enough though. This is the reason why you need to have good combat skills. On TV everything looks simple, but there is so much more to fighting than what you realize. Even a professional fighter never stops learning. It will come in handy if you take a class in mixed martial arts or combat self defense. With the right set of skills your size won't matter even if you have to take on a large attacker.

Weapons training

It is not enough to just own a firearm, you also need to know how to handle it in a safe manner, how to clean it, and how to also shoot with it with a good degree of accuracy. Hopefully it never comes to a situation where you have to use a firearm for your safety, but you need to be ready to use one if necessary. As with any other skill, you need to continuously practice. It is easier to miss an attacker than you probably think. You may only have a couple of seconds when someone is charging towards you. This would mean that you would have only a couple of seconds to draw your weapon and fire.

Keep the range of your firearm in your mind. The more experience you are at shooting the better is your chances of survival. If you consider that you are better with a knife, then you can learn about combat with a knife. But this needs to be done only in the case of necessity. Again, be sure to check any local laws that may restrict the size, type, or where weapons can be carried or owned. A weapon will do you no good if it is confiscated for illegal ownership.

First aid

You might have a first aid kit at home and even in your vehicle. Do you really know what you can do with all the items in it? You need to remember that hospitals may be flooded with wounded when a disaster strikes. This means that you will have to be able to provide at least the minimum first aid to any hurt friend, family member, or even yourself until you can get proper medical care. Suppose you are the one that has been hurt, then you should at least be in a position to give directions to others provided that you are still conscious. Take a class in first aid and ensure that you keep discarding any of the expired medicines in the first aid kit.

Being a handyman

Knowing how to fix things after or a disaster can be really helpful. There are several types of disasters that can cause serious damage to your house. Knowing basic plumbing, electrical, and carpentry skills can make all the difference between having a house to reside in and being forced to seek public shelter. Not just during the times of a disaster but also even during ordinary times, these skills will prove to be quite helpful.

Repairing equipment

Many people today don't really know how to fix things. This is the byproduct of a society in which it is much easier to replace a broken thing than to try and fix it. You just need to swipe your credit card and the item you liked will be delivered to your door. But there might come a time when you can't replace what is broken and you need to fix them like generators, flashlights, various appliances, or filtration systems. So, find all your repair manuals and try to learn how to fix such things.

Vehicle repair

Just like I have mentioned above, less and less people seem to know how to repair their vehicles. For learning to repair your vehicle you should get plenty of spare parts and learn how to install them. You might also want to learn how to hotwire a car. This isn't just a skill for criminals. It can help to provide an escape vehicle for yourself if you are stranded somewhere and have no other alternative. Knowing how to start an abandoned vehicle would be quite helpful.

Haggling

Once the economy collapses, there will be marketplaces sprouting up everywhere. Your day-to-day life will go on, but many people might not be able to afford to buy new things all over again. They might have to purchase used items or barter their items for something in return. If you happen to find yourself in such a situation having good haggling and negotiating skills will be helpful. These skills can be developed only by practice.

Conclusion

Thank you for buying this eBook! I hope this book proved to be informative and gave you an insight on what surviving is all about. Disasters not only wreck havoc but they also cause several inconveniences. You will find yourself cut from all the basic facilities that you are so used to. Prepping can be hard, but surviving is harder. So, it is really important that you prepare well in advance to face any adverse situations. It takes a fair amount of planning and preparation. You should keep conducting mock drills to make sure that you will be prepared. Make sure that you are mentally strong enough to deal with the survival situation and physically fit too.

This book provided you with an overview of disasters and different survival skills. Survival skills are extremely essential. Start prepping and planning, this is the only way you can survive any extreme situation. It is not just about acquiring knowledge about bushcraft and urban survival. You will need to put to practice what you have learned.

You need to remember that you are the only one who is responsible for your survival, you and no one else. Remember to stay calm, keep a positive attitude and the practical knowledge will help in your survival. Thank you once again for purchasing this book.

Instant Access to Free Book Package!

As a thank you for the purchase of this book, I want to offer you some more material. We collaborate with multiple other authors specializing in various fields. We have best-selling, master writers in history, biographies, DIY projects, home improvement, arts & crafts and much more! **We make a promise to you to deliver at least 4 books a week in different genres, a value of $20-30, for FREE!**

All you need to do is sign up your email here at http://nextstopsuccess.net/freebooks/ to join our Book Club. You will get weekly notification for more free books, courtesy of the First Class Book Club.

As a special thank you, we don't want you to wait until next week for these 4 free books. We want to give you 4 **RIGHT NOW**.

Here's what you will be getting:

1. A fitness book called "BOSU Workout Routine Made Easy!"
2. A book on Jim Rohn, a master life coach: "The Best of Jim Rohn: Lessons for Life Changing Success"
3. A detailed biography on Conan O'Brien, a favorite late night TV show host.
4. A World War 2 Best Selling box set (2 books in 1!): "The Third Reich: Nazi Rise & Fall + World War 2: The Untold Secrets of Nazi Germany".

To get instant access to this free ebook package (a value of $25), and weekly free material, all you need to do is click the link below:

http://nextstopsuccess.net/freebooks/

Add us on Facebook: First Class Book Club

www.ingramcontent.com/pod-product-compliance
Lightning Source LLC
Chambersburg PA
CBHW061944280526
45787CB00004B/1728